Cornerstones of Freedom

The Boston Tea Party

R. Conrad Stein

CHILDREN'S PRESS®
A Division of Grolier Publishing
New York • London • Hong Kong • Sydney
Danbury, Connecticut

Library of Congress Cataloging-in-Publication Data

Stein, R. Conrad.
 The Boston Tea Party / by R. Conrad Stein.
   p. cm.—(Cornerstones of freedom)
 Includes index.
 Summary: Describes the events preceding, during, and following
this noted event, which helped precipitate the American
Revolutionary War.
 ISBN 0-516-20005-4
 1. Boston Tea Party, 1773—Juvenile literature. [1. Boston Tea
Party, 1773. 2. United States—History—Revolution, 1775–1783—
Causes.] I. Title. II. Series.
E215.7.S83 1996
973.3'115—dc20
                                                  96-2082
                                                    CIP
                                                     AC

In 1763, bands blared patriotic songs in England and the American colonies. On both sides of the Atlantic Ocean, people danced in the streets to celebrate the end of the French and Indian War. In that conflict, the British, with help from the American colonists, achieved a glorious triumph.

For centuries, Europeans had established settlements in North America. By the 1700s, England had established thirteen colonies on the east coast of North America. After the French and Indian War, England claimed ownership of Canada and the region to the west of the thirteen colonies. It seemed the victory over the French would usher in a golden era for the British Empire in North America.

The French and Indian War ended in 1763.

England's Parliament imposed taxes on the colonies.

But the war had lasted seven years, and it had left Britain in debt. To rebuild its treasury, the British Parliament decided to tax the American colonies. The British government had never before imposed direct taxes on Americans. To members of Parliament, the decision to tax seemed to be a logical one. They believed that winning the French and Indian War benefitted the colonies. Besides, the American colonists were among the most prosperous people on

4

earth and would be able to afford to pay taxes. The colonists, however, were furious at the idea of paying

Colonists read the Stamp Act (left); angry citizens sometimes beat tax collectors (above).

taxes to the British. As colonists, they were not entitled to have representatives in Parliament to argue against taxation. The Americans cried out, "Taxation without representation is tyranny!" Those words later became a battle cry.

Ignoring the Americans' complaints, the British Parliament passed the Stamp Act in 1765. The act put a tax on newspapers, legal documents, and even playing cards. Outraged by the taxes, the colonists organized a boycott and refused to buy British-made goods. Tax collectors were jeered and sometimes even beaten.

Of all the colonial cities, Boston, Massachusetts, was the heart of anti-British feeling. Aware of this, the British government stationed two regiments of soldiers in the city in 1768. Authorities hoped that the presence of the

Citizens of Boston burn their tax notices to protest against the British government.

British troops arrive in Boston in 1768. Parliament hoped the troops would dispel anti-British feelings.

army would remind Bostonians that England's King George III was in control. Bostonians despised the red-jacketed soldiers and considered them unwelcome in their city.

On the snowy afternoon of March 5, 1770, a Boston crowd began taunting a British guard who was standing sentry duty in front of the customshouse. The customshouse served as the headquarters for British tax collectors. The crowd, some of whom had been drinking whiskey, began making fun of the guard's red jacket. "Lobster!" they shouted. "Bloody back, bloody back!" Reports say that a group of teenagers began pelting the guard with snowballs. The guard called for help. About twenty redcoats advanced to the customshouse with bayonets fixed on their rifles. The precise

Colonists sometimes made fun of the British soldiers.

Five Bostonians were killed in the Boston Massacre on March 5, 1770.

Crispus Attucks

details of what happened next are unknown. One soldier fired his weapon, perhaps by accident. The gunshot was followed by another, and another, and another. When the rifle smoke finally cleared, five Bostonians lay on the street, dead or dying. One of the dead was Crispus Attucks, an African-American man who lived in the city. Today many historians hail Attucks as the first casualty of the American Revolution.

News of the massacre spread through the colonies.

The tragic event that took place that day became known as the Boston Massacre. Bitter feelings quickly spread throughout the colonies when stories about the massacre appeared in newspapers. The Boston Massacre was the first major step in the colonies' long march toward the American Revolutionary War. Three years later, another inflammatory incident took place in Boston. That incident involved the colonists' favorite drink—tea.

Americans inherited their love of tea from the British. The drink was a social institution in the colonies, as it was in England. Guests in a person's home were almost always treated to a cup of hot tea. In 1770, Parliament reduced a series of taxes it had imposed earlier. But, significantly, Parliament decided to keep the tax on tea. The tea tax was kept largely as a symbolic gesture. The British government wanted to remind the colonists that it still held the power to tax its American possession.

The tax on tea angered the colonists. Many of them refused to buy tea imported from Great Britain. Women gave "non-tea" parties, during which they served only milk or fruit juice. Coffee became a popular alternative to tea. The city of Boston led the protest against the British tea tax.

In the colonies, tea was a very popular drink to serve at social occasions.

Samuel Adams

The most enthusiastic anti-British spokesman was an aging Bostonian named Samuel Adams. Born in Boston in 1722, Adams graduated from Harvard College in 1740 and prepared to enter the business world. But he was not successful as a businessman. He was chronically late for appointments. He had trouble with the figures and details connected with running a store or a bank. Day after day he wore the same wrinkled brown suit.

Abandoning his business career, Adams plunged into colonial politics. In politics, he was much more successful. He listened patiently to the problems of Boston's doctors, farmers, and laborers. During town meetings at the city's Faneuil Hall, Adams argued that the colonists should reject taxation without representation and demand the same rights that British citizens held. In time, he would begin to use an emotionally charged word that could send him to jail for treason—independence.

Adams worked tirelessly for the colonial cause. He organized supporters in Massachusetts into groups called the Committees of Correspondence. The committees were a letter-writing network intended to keep rural villages up-to-date on the latest news. Under Adams's direction, however, the network changed its focus. It began sending anti-British propaganda from town to town. Some eighty committees were formed in Massachusetts, and the practice soon extended to other colonies. Adams also supported the Boston chapter of the Sons of Liberty, a semisecret club

BOSTON, JUNE 22d, 1773.

SIR.

THE Committee of Correspondence of the Town of *Boston*, conformable to that Duty which they have hitherto endeavoured to discharge with Fidelity, again address you with a very fortunate important Discovery; and cannot but express their grateful Sentiments in having obtained the Approbation of so large a Majority of the Towns in this Colony, for their past Attention to the general Interest.

A more extraordinary Occurrence possibly never yet took Place in *America*; the providential Care of that gracious Being who conducted the early Settlers of this Country to establish a safe Retreat from Tyranny for themselves and their Posterity in *America*, has again wonderfully interposed to bring to Light the Plot that had been laid for us by our malicious and insidious Enemies.

Our present Governor has been exerting himself (as the honourable House of Assembly have expressed themselves in their late Resolves) " by his secret confidential Correspondence. to introduce Measures " destructive of our constitutional Liberty, while he has practiced every " method among the People of this Province, to fix in their Minds " an exalted Opinion of his warmest Affection for them, and his " unremitted Endeavours to promote their best Interest at the Court " of Great-Britain." This will abundantly appear by the Letters and Resolves which we herewith transmit to you; the serious Perusal of which will shew you your present most dangerous Situation. This Period calls for the strictest Concurrence in Sentiment and Action of every individual of this Province, and we may add, of THIS CONTINENT; all private Views should be annihilated, and the Good of the Whole should be the single Object of our Pursuit— " By uniting we stand," and shall be able to defeat the Invaders and Violaters of our Rights.

We are,

Your Friends and humble Servants,

Signed by Direction of the Committee for Correspondence in *Boston*,

William Cooper } *Town-Clerk.*

To the Town-Clerk of _____, to be immediately delivered to the Committee of Correspondence for your Town, if such a Committee is chosen, otherwise to the Gentlemen the Selectmen, to be communicated to the Town.

Letter from the Boston Committee of Correspondence

12

whose members also spoke of independence.

Adams formed a closely knit circle of friends, most of whom were anti-British. Today, a list of those friends reads like a patriots' Hall of Fame. The wealthy merchant John Hancock was an Adams associate. Hancock later signed the Declaration of Independence in larger-than-life handwriting so that King George III could read his signature without the aid of spectacles. Another friend of Samuel Adams was the talented silversmith, Paul Revere. At the dawn of the revolution, Revere became a legend by riding out of Boston in the middle of the night to warn rebellious colonists that the British army was on the march. At first, Samuel's cousin, John Adams, was reluctant to take an anti-British stand. But at the urging of his older relative, John, too, became an outspoken convert to the cause of independence. In 1796, John Adams was elected the second president of the United States.

John Adams

John Hancock (left) signed the Declaration of Independence (below).

The Sons of Liberty supported independence.

Although Samuel Adams had powerful friends, he failed to convince a majority of the colonists to support independence. By the 1770s, the colonists had enjoyed 150 years of harmonious relations with England. Most colonists considered themselves to be English, just like residents of British cities such as London or Liverpool. Loyal colonists denounced Adams and his associates as troublemakers.

The tea issue, however, struck a very sensitive nerve in the colonies. Actually, the tea tax cost a colonial family only a few pennies each year. But Americans resented taking orders from a higher authority. Every time they took a sip of tea, they imagined themselves under the control of a king who reigned over a country that was 3,000 miles (4,828 km) away.

The British East India Company headquarters

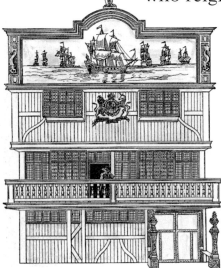

In 1773, England's Parliament made the already-tense situation worse by granting the British East India Company exclusive rights to sell tea in the colonies. The British government thus gave the company a monopoly in America. The monopoly meant the company could raise tea prices as high as it wished without fear of competition from other tea companies.

Samuel Adams knew the majority of colonists were not yet ready to push for independence from England. But the tea tax outraged almost everyone in the colonies. Adams knew that the angry citizens would begin to demand results.

Across the Atlantic Ocean, the British East India Company had no idea of the trouble occurring in the colonies. Late in the summer of 1773, the company sent a fleet of ships loaded with half a million pounds of tea to several American ports. One of those port cities was Boston.

When the tea ships were spotted off the Atlantic coast, the Committees of Correspondence sprang into action. Swift riders, including Paul Revere, carried news to colonial leaders of the vessels' approach. The leaders decided to try a new boycott tactic. Instead of simply declining to buy the tea once it was in the stores, they refused to unload it from the ships. In the port cities of Philadelphia and New York, the strategy worked.

Paul Revere alerted Bostonians when the tea ships arrived.

The British East India Company's ships returned to England with the tea still in their holds. The situation in Samuel Adams's Boston proved to be more complicated.

Royal Governor Thomas Hutchinson

A wealthy Bostonian named Thomas Hutchinson served as Royal Governor for the Massachusetts colony. He was American-born, from a distinguished family, and his sympathies were solidly behind the British crown. Aware of what happened in New York and Philadelphia, Hutchinson was determined that the tea ships now sailing toward Boston would be unloaded and all taxes would be paid. As Royal Governor he felt duty-bound to enforce British laws. But he had an additional motive for making sure the tea was properly distributed. Hutchinson's two sons worked for the British East India Company. His sons would make a large profit when the tea was sold in Boston.

While the ships were still at sea, Samuel Adams, John Hancock, and the Sons of Liberty held a spirited meeting at the Liberty Tree. The Liberty Tree was a stately old elm that stood in Boston's Hanover Square. The tree often served

Speakers rallied crowds against the British.

as a rallying point for anti-British speakers. At the meeting, one speaker after another cried out against the British taxes. A mob marched from the Liberty Tree to the

dockside. The people gathered in front of the British East India Company office, where they demanded that the company's agents come outside. The agents refused to meet with the protesters. Eventually, the angry Bostonians went home. Meanwhile, the ships sailed closer to Boston Harbor.

Abigail Adams

On November 11, 1773, the first of the tea ships, the *Dartmouth*, dropped anchor outside of Boston. During the next three weeks, two more tea ships, the *Eleanor* and the *Beaver*, arrived. The ships tied up at the wharf, but dockworkers refused to unload them. Several British warships were farther out in the harbor, their heavy guns pointed at the docks. Tension gripped the city.

In a house on Queen Street, John Adams's wife, Abigail, wrote, "The tea, that baneful weed, is arrived. . . . The flame is kindled, and like lightning it catches from soul to soul. . . . I tremble when I think what may be the direful

Boston Harbor

consequences, and in this town [Boston] must

the scene of the action lie. My heart beats at every whistle I hear, and I dare not express half my fears."

The tension between Governor Hutchinson and Samuel Adams escalated when Governor Hutchinson issued a deadline. Hutchinson declared that taxes on the tea aboard all three ships must be paid by midnight on December 16, 1773. If the taxes were not paid by that date, the governor would order the army to seize the ships and unload the cargo. As the deadline grew closer, citizens felt increasingly anxious.

December 16 was a cold, rainy day in Boston. But with the governor's deadline only a few hours away, a crowd of 7,000 people, the largest ever assembled in Boston's history, gathered at the Old South Church to attend a meeting organized by Samuel Adams. The gathering was so big that people spilled into the streets outside the church. Speakers addressed the throng. One by one they demanded that the ships return to England with their tea. With each speech, the people in the crowd grew more furious. Finally Samuel Adams climbed to the pulpit of the church and motioned for the crowd to be silent. He uttered ten fateful words: "This meeting can do nothing more to save the country." That statement triggered the crowd into action.

"To the wharf!" someone in the church shouted.

"Tonight the Boston Harbor is a teapot!"

Suddenly, from out of the church's back room came about fifty men. They were wrapped in blankets and disguised as Mohawk Indians. Most of the men had chimney soot or red "warpaint" smeared on their faces. They carried axes that they called "tomahawks." All of them were prominent and easily recognizable citizens of Boston. They hoped their Mohawk disguises would confuse British spies who might later testify against them in court. Encouraged by the presence of the "Mohawks," people throughout the church shouted and called each other to action.

Old South Church

"To the wharf! To the wharf!"

The crowd poured out of the Old South Church and began a march toward the city's docks. When they arrived at the dock area, the group became silent. All knew that British warships lurked in the dark waters. No one wanted to attract the attention of the British navy.

The colonists dressed as Mohawks split into three groups, one for each tea ship that was docked at the wharf. Quietly they climbed aboard the ships and summoned the crews. The leaders of each group ordered the crew members to open the cargo holds. The sailors complied without argument. The holds were jammed with chests of tea, each one weighing 320 pounds (145 kg). Using the ships' winches, the Mohawks hauled the chests up one by one. Once on deck, they broke open the chests and dumped the contents overboard. The British crews made no attempt to interfere. In fact, several sailors helped the colonists unload the tea.

Emptying the tea into Boston Harbor

One of those on deck was a teenager named Robert Sessions. Years later Sessions wrote, "I was not one of those appointed to destroy the tea, and who disguised themselves as Indians, but was a volunteer, the disguised men being largely men of family and position in Boston." Sessions said that other young men who were onlookers such as himself readily joined in the protest. "Perfect regularity prevailed during the whole transaction. Although there were many

people on the wharf, entire silence prevailed—no clamor, no talking. Nothing was meddled with but the teas on board."

The only casualty came when a winch broke and struck a twenty-nine-year-old carpenter named John Crane. Crane was knocked unconscious, and many thought he was killed by the blow. But mindful of British warships, the colonists continued unloading the ships. Crane was carried to the docks and put on a bed of wood shavings. Later his friends returned to find him dazed but very much alive.

The colonists dumped 342 chests of tea into Boston Harbor.

23

Every remnant of the tea was dumped overboard.

A short time later, the colonists had dumped all 342 chests of tea into the harbor. Reports claimed that one of the men attempted to steal a portion of the tea by stuffing it into his pockets. As punishment, he was stripped of his clothes to be sure he could not steal any more tea, and sent home. Before the colonists left the ships, they swept the decks clean. They wanted to be sure that every remnant of tea had been dumped into the harbor.

Their work completed, the colonists marched into the night. When they were safely out of the range of British guns, smiles and laughter broke

The Tea Party may have been planned in this building.

out among them. Colonists named their protest the Boston Tea Party. Someone took a fife from his pocket and played a lively version of "Yankee Doodle." A few days later, a patriot wrote a song that became a popular hit throughout the thirteen colonies. It was sung to the tune of "Yankee Doodle."

Rally, Mohawks! Bring out your axes,
And tell King George we'll pay no taxes
On his foreign tea.

When word of the Boston Tea Party arrived in faraway London, King George and the members of England's Parliament were not amused. The British government decided to close the port of Boston and placed all of Massachusetts under military control. Colonists called this

The First Continental Congress met in Carpenter's Hall in Philadelphia.

punishment the "Intolerable Acts." Stirred by anger over the Intolerable Acts, delegates from twelve other colonies formed the First Continental Congress and agreed to end trade with England. It was the first time that the colonies unified to protest a British law.

The Boston Tea Party set in motion a long chain of events that ultimately led to American independence. Dumping the tea defied British law. The punishment imposed on Boston by British authorities made the colonists even more angry. Sixteen months later the Revolutionary War began at Lexington and Concord outside of Boston. The war continued for eight long years. Yet the upheaval resulted in the birth of the United States of America. In 1776, while the war was still being fought, Thomas Jefferson wrote the Declaration of Independence. Four years after the war ended, American delegates signed the United States Constitution. This document served as the basis for the new nation's government. Patriot leaders considered the Boston Tea Party to be the catalyst for the Revolution and the long march toward independence. Writing at the time, John Adams said, "The die is cast. The people have passed the river and cut away the bridge. . . . This [the Boston Tea Party] is the grandest event that has yet happened since the controversy with Britain was opened. The sublimity of it charms me."

While the Boston Tea Party was the first major protest by colonial Americans against the British, actual fighting on April 19, 1775, began the Revolutionary War. British soldiers and colonial militiamen fought in the towns of Lexington and Concord, Massachusetts. The war continued for eight more years, until 1783, when the United States of America was finally free from British rule.

GLOSSARY

baneful – full of harm

boycott – refusal to buy or use specific goods as an act of protest

chronically – constantly; habitually

direful – frightening; dreadful

hold – ship's interior; place below deck where cargo is stored

inflammatory – intended to provoke anger

institution – firmly established custom; tradition

intolerable – unacceptable; unbearable

loyalist – person who clings to a cause or remains loyal to a monarch or government

monopoly – exclusive ownership or control

Parliament – governing body in Britain composed of representatives selected by the people

propaganda – ideas, facts, or rumors spread to further a person's or group's cause

protesters – people who speak or act against an issue

stately – majestic; dignified

sublimity – understated power

symbolic – object or action that represents another idea

taunt – to jeer or mock a person or persons

treason – betrayal of a person's government

winch – machine used to lift heavy objects

protesters

taunt

TIMELINE

French and Indian War ends **1763**

1765

British Parliament
passes Stamp Act

Parliament stations soldiers in Boston **1768**

March 5: Boston Massacre **1770**

1772 Samuel Adams establishes Committees
of Correspondence

1773

1774 Parliament passes Intolerable Acts

1775 *April 19:* Revolutionary War begins

1776 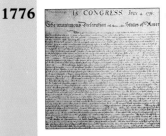 *July 4:*
Declaration of
Independence
signed

Summer:
East India
Company sends
tea ships to
colonies; dock-
workers refuse
to unload tea

Early Winter:
Tea ships arrive
in Boston
Harbor

December 16:
Boston Tea Party

1783 Revolutionary War ends

1787 United States Constitution signed

INDEX *(**Boldface** page numbers indicate illustrations.)*

PHOTO CREDITS

©: Cover, Stock Montage, Inc.; 1, North Wind Picture Archives; 2, Stock Montage, Inc.; 3, The Bettmann Archive; 4, North Wind Picture Archives; 5 (both photos), Stock Montage, Inc.; 6, The Bettmann Archive; 7, 8, North Wind Picture Archives; 9 (top), The Bettmann Archive; 9 (bottom right), Stock Montage, Inc.; 10, 11 (both photos), 12, North Wind Picture Archives; 13 (top right), 13 (bottom left), The Bettmann Archive; 13 (bottom right), AP/Wide World Photos; 14 (both photos), 15, North Wind Picture Archives; 16 (both photos), The Bettmann Archive; 17, Stock Montage, Inc.; 18 (top left), AP/Wide World Photos; 18 (bottom), American Antiquarian Society; 20, 21, 22, 23, 24, North Wind Picture Archives; 25, Culver Pictures Inc.; 26, American Antiquarian Society; 27, 29, North Wind Picture Archives; 30 (top), The Bettmann Archive; 30 (bottom), North Wind Picture Archives; 31 (top right), Stock Montage, Inc.; 31 (bottom left), North Wind Picture Archives; 31 (bottom right), AP/Wide World Photos

ABOUT THE AUTHOR

R. Conrad Stein was born and raised in Chicago. After serving in the Marine Corps he attended the University of Illinois, where he received a degree in history. He later studied in Mexico, then returned to Chicago and became a full-time writer. Mr. Stein is the author of more than eighty books, articles, and short stories for young readers. His works for Children's Press include *The Assassination of Martin Luther King Jr.*, *The California Gold Rush*, *The Declaration of Independence*, and *The Pilgrims*. Mr. Stein lives in Chicago with his wife and their daughter, Janna.